EMOTIONAL INTELLIGENCE

"The breakup book"

How to get over breakup anxiety and live your life

KATHERINE ABBOTT

Also by Katherine Abbott

'Spiritual Candy' blog:
www.spiritual-candy.com

Spiritual_Candy:

Instagram

Facebook

Twitter

Pinterest

Get the free

**"Awaken your Dreams"
video course and tools**

by signing up to the Spiritual Candy community

www.spiritual-candy.com/free-video-course/

Disclaimer
Important note...

All information in this book is entirely my personal knowledge, experience and opinion and is intended for personal development purposes only. These pages are not to be taken as medical advice but as spiritual information. I am not, and do not claim to be a medical doctor, therapist or licensed mental health professional. If you have a health problem, please see a Doctor or other appropriate professional. Any information received here should not be used in place of professional medical and/or psychological treatment. You alone are responsible for any of your choices, your decisions and your actions in life. All content is for entertainment purposes only and those under the age of 18 should not follow these steps, except with adult supervision.

EMOTIONAL INTELLIGENCE

"The breakup book"

How to get over breakup anxiety and live your life

KATHERINE ABBOTT

Contents

"You are so Loved"

Introduction

We all face heartache and break. However, this guide is for that gut wrenching, hideous, breathtaking, damaging heartache pain that makes you feel as if you will never recover. I am an empath, intuitive and have done countless intuitive readings on every topic you can imagine. However, by far my biggest question is: how to deal with, get over or improve heartbreak. I get crisis calls from all different people from all sorts of walks of life. It seems to be a universal problem and a massive call to me to reach out and help those who ask me on a weekly basis... how do I deal with this heartbreak?

This is a pick me up, a lift and a 'kick start'. It is quite simply my experience of *what worked for me* and an account of *how I overcame the struggle*. It is what I have advised others to do and have found it works. It is the hope that it will be a friend to you or someone in a similar situation- that you will remember and connect with your deeper sense again- that you will remember that you are so loved. If you are in a painful situation, you are not alone in your problem. It is good to know that someone else got through it and you can and will too. To hear someone else describe your struggle and say what they did to come through it can be most encouraging if you feel you don't know where to turn. I did this and this is my chance to 'pass it on'. Books have always represented for me hope, growth and support and my wish is that this book provides that service to someone else.

I am a recovering co-dependent who has had abusive style relationships, many dysfunctional relationships and spent her whole 20s and early 30s doubled up in pain and grief over men. My 'love de jour' was always the centre of my world and my singular obsession. I was always totally captivated and mesmerised by him; he was my 'everything'. Whilst I have been and always will be a lover- it is inherent in my nature- I always took it too far. Somewhat trained, also self encouraged; I made the man in my life the centre of the world.

Don't get me wrong, it is great to serve and to love but it was at largely the exclusion of all other things, including myself.

My ferocity of passion and commitment was also in direct correlation to how much I needed my man. I just couldn't be a real and whole person without them because I was so outward focused. If I didn't have a guy telling me I was ok, how would I know? If he wasn't telling me what I looked like, how could I know what to wear? Now, please understand, I was a somewhat extreme example. I am not suggesting that you are struggling to pick a sweater or shirt just because you are now without that particular person, but you get the idea of what I'm trying to say here?

If you are stuck in heartbreak, there is more than just loss of companionship going on here and the relationship was perhaps providing a different service as well as the traditional one. In order to get past the pain, we have to delve in to that to understand it and heal. This short book aims to encapsulate the basics of what got me started on an upwards trajectory. These are the things that worked for me and I am sharing them in the hope that they may help you too.

"Make the effort
and make the
change"

The Basics

*T*his short book aims to make a proper dent into your sadness and move you further along your healing path. To keep it simple, it is a fourteen day programme that aims to make a difference in a short time. Is it an answer to everything? No, of course not but, if you follow the steps closely, it should give you insight to get you from where you are towards where you want to be. There is no magic wand to get over heartache but it doesn't need to be an impossible task either.

Introduction to The Steps

To start with you need an hour or so to go through steps 1-8

Once you have read through and digested the 8 steps, you need to make a commitment to put these things in place. They can all be done in one day. However, if you want to take a few days to get yourself ready before you start the 13 day challenge; that is fine.

I want to give you a few brief warnings here...

1. This programme will only work if you do it- all of it.
2. It will not be easy
3. It will not magically get better...

You have to want to get past the pain and be determined to do so.

So, in short, you've got to get in there with the right attitude. My guess is that a lot of people may read the 8 steps, put some of it in place and then fail to really follow through. I know this because this is what I did over and over again. I cannot and will not criticise you or this book if you don't manage to get there because I didn't for a long time.

But, don't be like me!

Don't take repeating the same pattern with different faces over and over before you recognise what is going on. Make the effort and make the change. Whilst I know this book works and works well, it is the quick start challenge that will get you out of that rut and move you forwards. But, it will not have all of your relationship riddles solved and sorted in two weeks. You are going to have to continue to help yourself move along; to grow and evolve in whatever way feels good for you.

"If you want a partner to love, respect and honour you, you first have to do this for yourself."

The Steps:

1. Get as healthy as possible.

"This seems like such an obvious point and yet it is one that I believe is often massively underrated when it comes to mental and emotional health."

Y ou are going to aim to make space to get enough sleep, drink plenty of water, keep your eating and drinking habits as clean as possible and get some exercise. All of the things that create a healthy mind and body, you must now employ. However, please be sensible and moderate.

Now, in your pain, is not the time to force yourself to give up sugar, stop a life-long habit (please read the disclaimer!) or take on a new gruelling work out scheme necessarily. I am asking you to look at your own life and notice how healthy you can comfortably go without making major lifestyle changes. Go to that level you're at and maybe just a little healthier still. For example, if up until now you have not been healthy at all, I am asking that you add in some healthy fruit and vegetables, that you make sure you get outside for some fresh air each day and take at least a 15 minute walk if nothing else. I ask that you keep your unhealthy habits to a minimum and that you take the best care of yourself that you can.

If you are already doing something, try to improve it; make some sort of positive addition to your daily routine and habits...

"You need your strength and mental acuity now as you take on this situation. In getting over your heartache, you are going to be breaking an old habit and

trying to create a new one. For some of us, particularly if we are not used to challenging and disciplining ourselves in this way, it will be really hard. Therefore, you need your body well fuelled in all senses of the word in order to have the best chance of success."

If you are feeling really down or are struggling with any areas of your life and you have bad physical habits regarding your health, this is something to really consider thinking about once you are back on track and out of this relationship rut. Being fit and healthy in the body reflects in your mind and emotions and vice versa. So, once you are feeling better this is a great place from which to continue to build better health and circumstances.

Keep in mind that whilst being healthy just makes doing things, being on form and generally doing well in life much easier, it is also a symbol of how you treat and think of yourself. If you don't take care of yourself, this sends a massive signal out in to the universe of how others and the world should treat you too. If you want a partner to love, respect and honour you, you first have to do this for yourself. You must look after yourself in every way, it starts with the fuel you put into your body and how you take care of yourself.

"The problem is when
we lie to ourselves and
believe it."

2. Face the pain

"Your pain may not feel like heartbreak in a conventional way, particularly if you have been very hurt before. It might present as apathy, emptiness or numbness rather than tears, sadness and grief. However, if you are struggling to imagine a new relationship or feel in any way aware of being torn up over a relationship, let's just call it heartbreak, for now at least."

I know that my reaction was often to try and just forget it and keep myself busy. Going in to a heavy denial over the pain may seem, to the outside world and even those who love you the most, like a good thing.

It may even be something that is encouraged; a "fake it till you make it" type of an attitude. In doing this you become that "strong person", getting on with life and giving two metaphorical fingers to the toe-rag who hurt you. But, heavy denial often comes with massive ramifications. Heavy denial can easily drive the pain deep inside and can come out in all sorts of weird ways. Let me be clear; it will come out. It always does.

I have been a primary school teacher and mentor and one of the things I have said and heard many times is

'You know the truth will come out, it always does!'

I tried to teach children this in order that they learn to be authentic and honest with themselves. Whether they maintain 'the lie' about who took the pen when they shouldn't have done, is not that relevant. After all, we all tell lies to others to avoid a difficult conversation or to get ourselves out of hot water. The problem is when we lie to ourselves and believe it.

This is when our pain starts to manifest itself in strange ways that 'don't make sense' to us. The denial tells us that we 'aren't bothered' by what's happened. Therefore we are perplexed by our bodies acting out or things start becoming confused. We have detached ourselves from our feelings and so our body's or mind's reaction makes no sense and has no conscious 'cause'. We need to make that link and allow ourselves to feel what we feel and reclaim the feeling or wound. If we don't attend to the wounds they will perhaps not get better, repeat themselves or, as I said before, manifest themselves as a problem that seems to have 'no obvious cause'.

Many of our elders have told us that time heals all wounds and this can sometimes give us encouragement to 'let sleeping dogs lie' and not face up properly to what has happened. Well, perhaps time does heal on some occasions, but for me it really wasn't because the wound magically healed itself. In my case, it was because of the combination of the steps I offer in this book and me diligently sticking to them (well mostly, anyway). So, don't run. Be careful ignoring the problem because, unless something circumstantial distracts us, we may find that, even years later, we are still waiting to recover. In reality, very few of us are going to avoid a heartbreak of some sort or other. If we can face and accept it, we will be able to do something about it.

"Be brutally honest. You then know that you have been heard"

3. Tell the story honestly.

*W*hat are you telling yourself? What happened? What were all of the gut wrenching details? Again, rather like the previous step, some of you may feel or have been encouraged to 'leave it be' and not talk it though. However, in my experience,

"...you may need to tell your story authentically and honestly."

I think free writing, where you just allow it all to come out on the page uninterrupted, is really helpful but this might not work for you. Whatever you do- whether it is writing, talking or painting (to name a few ways)- get your story out.

Really familiarise yourself with what it did, how you felt, what you wondered about it all and all your fears, worries and concerns. It may be good to tell a sympathetic and open friend.

Now this next thing is a bit controversial but, in my experience it is key....

There is something that, with few exceptions in my research, we all do when we have had our heart broken.

It is that one thing we turn over in our head and occasionally allow to slip out of our lips to a trusted friend in a fit of tears or rage.

The question is:

"Is there anything I could have done differently?"

I encourage you to discuss this with your friend or with yourself on paper. This may sound a strange thing to do but we are getting real. We are taking this problem by the scruff of the neck and sorting it out. We are not coming back here so we need to do all we can to satisfy, to some extent, our mind's questioning.

Let's be honest, we all think 'what could I have done differently?' and this often gives us an excuse to either keep going over it or, worse still, go back to the person and try to work it out/ get closure/ understand. The idea of consciously going over this methodically is that, by taking the time to tell your story honestly and think it all through, you are making doubly sure that everything is out in the open- to yourself that is.

Once you have done this, you are clear; everything you might want to let out, consider or discuss has been done, either with yourself, on paper or with a friend or therapist. Be warned though, part of your mind will always want to return and will never be done thinking it over. That is why we are thinking about it thoroughly now; this way, in a month's time when something reminds you and you start to ask yourself those questions again, you can be strict with yourself and say, "No, we've already discussed this and done all we can here. This case is closed!"

By being really honest and committing genuinely to how you really do feel and where you really are at, you have created a solid platform on which to start building. So, don't dance around it all. Be brutally honest. You then know you have been heard. You have aired it all and nothing is left unsaid or unprocessed. You are free to move.

"If we read too much into the pain or wait for the pain to go before we move forwards, this can actually just keep us stuck there"

4. Ignore the pain

*T*his sounds like craziness but it works! I realise that I have just asked you to be honest and face the pain, now I'm asking you to ignore it.

There is method in this.

You need to acknowledge the pain that you've been though and what has hurt you. You need to be clear about it. However, if you are heartbroken and here wanting a solution, one would assume you feel somewhat 'stuck' in a love for someone who is no longer available. Perhaps you have decided he or she is not right to be with or vice versa. Regardless, if you are completely in love with another, trying to 'get rid' of it will probably not work.

"Thousands of poems, songs, stories and historical accounts will tell you that, since the beginning of time, people have very little control over their so called 'heart's decisions' and desires."

People have and will continue to give up their health, wealth, home and sanity in the pursuit of love. It seems necessary then to accept that, sometimes, we just have to accept the way we feel about another and move forwards anyway. In step three, the pain was addressed and dealt with (as much as it can be) and so now is the time to accept what is left over and move on anyway.

So often, when we decide or have it decided for us that a relationship is over, we believe that it should be able to be entirely dealt with, signed off and packed away within a matter of days. This isn't realistic. This is one of the reasons I got stuck in the grieving of a relationship. I was reading too much into the pain or waiting for the pain to go before I moved forwards. This actually just kept me stuck there.

Here was a big reality check for me that brought me clarity, ease and relief:

"Still feeling sadness, pain or deep love is not a reason to believe this person is meant for you"

Listen and consider that point.

I'm not saying that the person you are considering is or isn't for you but I have heard so many times (and felt myself) this sense of connection and pain being used as an excuse to try and salvage or reinstate the relationship or 'wait' for some sort of 'revelation' on the other's part.

Whether that person is right for us or not, if we have a dysfunctional connection to them (and this is pretty common in my experience), it is going to be difficult to get over and disconnect from. This is something we need to accept.

If we are feeling a lot of love or pain, ruminating on this will not help us at this time. You do not need to feel a sense of resolution. In fact you probably won't *feel* a resolution at all at this stage but step 3 means you will *know* you are resolved. So, remind yourself that you have already gone over everything. For now at least, they are not around. So, we are going to move forwards. We do this at this stage by ignoring the residual pain.

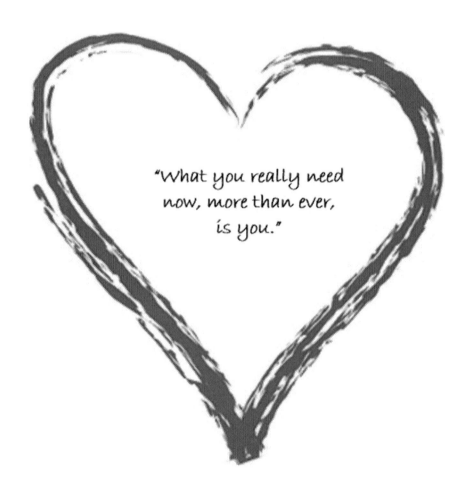

"What you really need
now, more than ever,
is you."

5. Get over the illusion and recognise what you need.

*L*et's start with the title of step 5. 'Get over the illusion'. What is the illusion? The illusion is the noise and cries your pain makes over your heartbreak. As I said in step 4, you will want to go back, think over, talk over or wonder about the pain if you are 'stuck' in it and your mind will quite probably want to go back to the person or at least back to the subject of what happened.

You cannot do this.

You must let it go.

You must discipline yourself.

"The idea that the solution lies with the relationship or the other is the illusion."

The difficulty in moving forwards from the sense of grief and 'stuck-ness' often times comes down to your willingness to accept this last statement. It isn't the other, what happened or why that matters now. Any thoughts around this are, quite possibly, illusory.

For some, it will not be easy to accept this. On many occasions I would not believe this and caved in to my base and dysfunctional egoic needs, by returning to the thoughts (or the actual person) looking for a solution; looking for something that would make me feel better. But this is- more often than not- not where the solution lies. You need to be strong, determined and wilful. You have to be able to ignore your pain's cries.

Don't use pain as an excuse to rake over it.

What you really need is you. What instigated my change was absolute frustration at being at the mercy of another (a partner) and the realisation that they could not fulfil the need that I had anyway.

In my case, I was not just sad because I had lost a great friend and someone who I shared a lot of time with. I was devastated because I felt I had lost part of myself and some of my hopes and dreams. Herein lied the illusion; the illusion that my satisfaction and happiness could be found in another. This was not at all true of course and was something that, once I realised and fully 'got', turned my situation around.

Something to think about...

My friend is a smart, young and beautiful woman who had a medium term relationship with a guy who messed her around and hardly valued her at all. She broke up with him after some disagreement about whether they would live in her place or his in the long term. It was a silly fight but was an excuse to end a difficult relationship. She wanted him to be bothered; he wasn't really. A year later, my friend, a teacher has moved to America and is teaching elementary school there. She has a new set of friends, has been dating a new and wonderful guy and generally is ridiculously happy. That is until the middle of the night last week when her lovely ambivalent ex called her on the phone and said how he missed her.

She is coming back to the UK for Christmas and he wants to see her. I heard all this on a Skype catch up earlier this week. Her response was "I'm probably going to meet up with him, I mean, I feel I probably should and maybe I just need it for some closure." I tried to hide my disbelief. Really? You haven't seen the guy for a year, he was never bothered about you, he has lots of dates and one proper girlfriend in the interim and you now live on the other side of the world but you need 'closure'

She doesn't need closure; she is living in the illusion.

She is still, in some way in her mind, still attached to him. She still loves him, still wants him and uses these things as excuses to see him. His calling and her feelings add up to a 'sign' to go towards him. What has really happened here? The wound of their breakup was never really healed. Her needs and unfulfilled desires have not been attended to. She has a longing that she thinks he can maybe solve. But, in truth only she can solve it. This is the *real* problem: we row in the wrong direction but moving towards the issue will not get you away from the issue. This has to make sense!

My belief is that I moved towards the pain, rather than away, time and time again because:

  a. I wanted it all to make total sense and to be clean and easy before 'moving on' (but it isn't always possible)
  b. I was misunderstanding the pain: I didn't realise that my pain was an indicator of where I needed to love and help me, not where the other had 'messed up' or not given enough.

Truth be told, I didn't want to feel the pain of it all being left undone and messy. I didn't want to admit that I had been left ripped open and no amount of reconstruction or discussion can change the facts of it. In short, I didn't want to face up to the truth of the events. I wanted to look again, to see if it maybe no longer hurt, to see if I could finally relax and find out that it had all 'magically healed'. It just wasn't going to happen.

"I didn't realise that everything I wanted to find and get from the other was actually an invitation to get it from myself."

I believe that my beautiful friend is in a similar level of denial. However, I (and maybe my friend too) was not educated in self fulfilment from an early age and, when I was faced with such pain, I got scared and did not know what to do with it. When the relationship broke, my answer was to try and fix it instead of noticing what it told me about myself and my relationship with me.

Being honest with yourself means you can avoid that constant return, either in reality or in your mind, to the scene of the devastation.

Going back to the source of the pain, the rejection, the hurt or the sadness, will not help you.

This isn't a blame game by the way, I'm not saying whether or not the other caused the pain...

Whatever happened, it ended.

Chances are that, if you are here reading this, at this time it is not easily, if at all, reconcilable. Be realistic. Be sensible and be brutal too. You are going to want to go back either in your mind or in reality and this is why step 2 is so vital. If you have told your story earnestly and investigated it properly then you have no excuse to go back. What you have to tell yourself, quite clearly and strongly, is that having a feeling and thought you want to go back does not mean that you should or that it is something sensible or reasonable.

Your head, mindful to avoid pain, will look for a quick fix and a simple way to get past the pain. If you are reading this, I suspect that it is telling you that the answer may be there with the other. It just most times isn't true. Accept what you need now is you. These things you want from the other; they can and should come from you. This is how to crush the illusion and recognise what you can do for you. Then we are ready to start rebuilding.

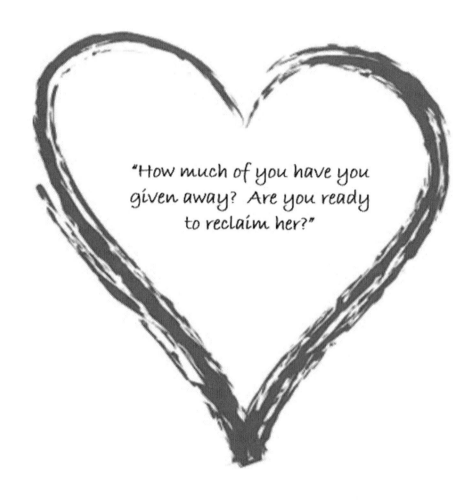

"How much of you have you given away? Are you ready to reclaim her?"

6. "Needing"

Recognise the difference between needing for the joy of connection and needing for self definition.

*F*or a very long time I have been turning this point over in my head, researching and wondering.

One expert says 'you don't need a partner to be happy' whilst another says 'you have to be vulnerable and 'need' a partner'.

It hit me when I was riding on the train and contemplating my relationship life- I have always been fixated on the term 'needing' and deciding whether I ought to really 'need' a partner or not. But what I really *needed* to do was really understand what I meant by *needing*.

It isn't that we need others that's the problem; we all need others, we're social animals. However, needing in order to be a fully functioning person is a problem. This is when we feel that person is part of who we are. This then becomes a real problem when the person is no longer there (and when they are there too, in actual fact). Not to misunderstand, if you have been with a person a very long time and then break up, you will probably feel an immense gap and loneliness for a short time. You will perhaps have a sense of not knowing what to do with yourself. This is very different to feeling that you don't know who you are anymore.

"If what you wear, think, do or believe is dependent on your partner in any way shape or form- when he or she goes then who are you? You are no longer a whole person. You may even feel you are empty and lost, 'identity-less.' This was me."

You may or may not feel that this point is relevant for you. I have to say that, in many instances, I have found it to be true and pretty much all of my 'heartache' I can attribute to this malfunction with my sense of identity.

Nowadays, I do not need anyone else to define me and I am fully functioning and happy as an individual. I know what I need to operate in my day successfully, I know my strengths, my weaknesses, where I need support, who I can turn to and how to connect to those around me. I am not completely 'dependent' on someone for direction or a sense of self and this is crucial and key.

Before you think 'this is definitely not me', understand that I was never an obvious co-dependent and it took me *forever* to recognise just how emotionally dependent I was. I had a business; I lived alone, functioned well and took care of those around me. I had a good job, responsibilities- from my dogs to taking care of my nephew- but still I was only partly 'me'. I was not entirely self-determined. This meant that I 'needed' a partner to feel like I knew how to be. I built my life around them and theirs and without it, I was like a climbing plant with nothing to climb up.

Nowadays, when I have a break up, I am hurt, in pain and sad. I feel a sense on a Saturday night of a gap and may cry as I sit alone. This is normal and natural. I also know that I am still me, everything is still the same inside of me and I will get used to the other's absence.

I miss them for a while but it goes away. I am no longer devastated and lost because I have only lost the partner not myself. Now, if you are feeling in any way the way I used to feel- stuck, confused, alone and lost- you may well find that some of your identity was placed on being that other person's partner or at least dependent on their presence in your life. There needs to be some reclaiming and re-establishing of who you are as a whole and total person. However, before you do this (and you'll find strategies in points 7 and 8 as to how I rebuilt my sense of self) a big part of the hurdle is recognising and acknowledging that this **is** what has happened. It may not be to the extent that I experienced but be mindful that any loss of identity needs to be taken back.

I needed to realise that I had lost a part of my identity.

I had given myself away and, with her, my opportunity to be the complete power and source of love, happiness and peace in my own life.

I had put my essence in someone else's hands.

I ask you to really digest this and contemplate how much of yourself you have given away and how. This step cannot be rushed. It took me some time to realise that this is what had happened and that I had the power to change it all. Without seeing this step, you may not be convinced that you can change your circumstances and belief is everything, as we well know. So, allow yourself to see where you are dependent and where this sense of emptiness and gap lies within you.

"Even if you are not convinced yet, be open to the possibility that you, with the grace of universal energy within you, can fill, heal, gather and re-piece this situation."

As a footnote to this step, you must be open to the possibility that you may not actually feel convinced that you can fill this void yourself until it has happened. I only truly recognised what was happening and that this method I'm outlining here had cured my dependence and heartbreak, when it had already happened. In fact, I wasn't doing steps 7 and 8 to cure my heart break at all; it was just a happy coincidence.

So, even if you are sceptical about having any co-dependent traits (this isn't saying you are actually a full blown 'co-dependent), just be willing to consider that perhaps you do. With acceptance, you can fill this gap and cure this longing. However long you've had it and however much of a pattern it may have become, it can be done. Be willing to try and above all else, act- act on the suggestions and commit to the process.

"Be open to the possibility that you, with the grace of universal energy within you, can fill, heal, gather and re-piece this situation."

"How much of you
have you given away? Are
you ready
to reclaim her?"

7. Getting practical

Who are you and what do you want to do?

*I*f you suffer with a strong sense of loss of identity, you will need to spend a good while on this exercise. Conversely, you might think you aren't reliant on your old partner for your identity and feel very strong and certain. However, you need to consider that, if your heart aches and you cannot control it, perhaps you have unknowingly lost a bit of yourself in the process of it all, without really realising it.

The important thing to focus on, once you have gone through points 1-6, is how to rebuild and create something additional to and alongside your pain or sadness or loss.

We have not and are not going to try and eradicate the old pain.

We are going to create something else to move across to.

Trying to take away loss is impossible.

Loss is by virtue a sense of lack so, by trying to get rid of it, we may well feel an even greater sense of emptiness than we felt before.

In fact, on several occasions, I believe that I held on to the memory and the pain just to keep a little of the relationship in my life. Without that, I really did have nothing of that 'old me'. So, we are not going to take anything else away in terms of this old relationship or the source of the heartbreak.   Instead we are going to just leave it where it is and metaphorically just put it in a box to the side for a short while whilst we move on to point 7.

Point 7 is the key moment, the turning point and the main advice for getting unstuck (in my opinion).

It does not involve the ex, thinking about him/her or the situation, going over anything or getting rid of any feelings or thoughts about him or her.

It is all about you.

Who are you?

What is it about you that makes you unique?

What are you habits, you desires, your hobbies and passions?

We are going to build your sense of worth, esteem and self beyond that which you already embrace.

Now, before you say anything or roll your eyes, I want you to just listen to something.   I have worked with so many clients and have had intuitive advice that basically *always* advises this point.   It seems to be the universal answer to pretty much everything.

Point 7 is a cure all.

It works; it works like a miracle.

It gives you everything you could imagine and more, and yet almost no one ever really does it (myself included- for **many** years).

Lots of people will consider it, they might even write a list or make a vision board but, by the next day, they have forgotten all about it and are back listening to the pain again.

You are going to step fully into you and do it every day- Consistently

The advice to get out of that stuck place is so simple it is ridiculous but it is not at all easy. It requires commitment and determination. You have to make your extensive list (which I'll explain below), get the physical practical things you need together and then show up every day for 14 days, regardless of the pain or sadness that tries to snap at your heels. As I said, it is very simple but will not be easy. You can do it but you will have to try really hard and focus like crazy. You will need to be determined and strong minded. There is no easy way. Waiting for the easy option is just putting off the inevitable. There is no easy option but there is a solution.

Listen to this truth: recovering, if you have felt stuck for a while, may not be easy. In fact it probably will feel tough and you are going to have to be like a firm but loving parent with yourself here. So, take your computer, paper or whatever you want to write on and get your list of who and what you are.

What are your greatest accomplishments?

What are you proud of?

What are your skills?

What do you contribute to other people's lives?

What are you good at?

What are your best traits?

What do you love to do?

How do you best express your love, joy and talent?

What are you interested in?

What do you admire?

Look at other people (real, famous or imaginary) that you appreciate and consider what it is about them that you would like to see in yourself? You see, if you believe it, you can be it. Oftentimes, in my experience, you tend to admire (and dislike, but that's for another book!) qualities in others that are hidden deep within yourself. So, now it's time to really outline your biggest and best self.

Expect to cringe or squirm a little, to feel like the ideas you want for yourself may be a little 'big' for you; that's ok and all part of the process. The important thing is to get a full and comprehensive sense of who and what you are, in your fullest totality. Don't worry that it will forever slightly shift and change. This picture of self will develop over time. Equally, don't worry if you feel you are struggling to see the total picture of yourself. Just see what you can for now knowing that you are doing just fine.

Now look at what you've outlined and, every day, work towards that.

Every day, do something that moves you towards that vision.

Every day, start to leave behind the things that don't line up with your vision.

Step fully into you and do it every day- Consistently

"Make your box of tricks;
bring
your soul self
to life"

8. Make your box of tricks

Your box of tricks is a practical version of point 7.

Where point 7 makes you aware of who and what you are, point 8 is a collection of tools to help you live actively in that person.

So, for example, if you realise that you used to love to paint and this is part of who you are, you might get out your old equipment, set up a painting area or just buy a small sketch pad to start sketching ideas in. If you realise that you pay no attention to yourself anymore and you want to be the kind listener to your own self and needs, you might buy a diary in order to listen to and record your thoughts each day.

You might compile a list of songs that uplift you or make a vision board of clippings to look at. You might take yourself out for the day or evening or take time to reminisce on your younger days and times when you were perhaps more connected to your original, creative, self aware nature. You might find that certain TV shows, lectures or educational books or recordings will help you or you may decide to take up a new hobby. Whatever it is that you have listed in point 7, point 8 is your physical actions to support and grow the person you are and want to grow in to over the coming two weeks. So, collect together all that you are going to need to step more into yourself and prepare for your 14 day plan.

List anything you need:

"And then she
Stood tall and
conquered"

The 14 Day Plan Introduction

*W*hatever you do, once you have gone through the eight steps, I would urge you not to try to talk about or think deeply about how this has moved you beyond the old partnership. It is tempting, if you make any progress away from the sadness, to get carried away with the enjoyment of the release and seeming escape from the 'stuckness' you used to feel. However thinking about it, even in this way, can in itself be a trap that you don't want to fall in to. The reason to not go over the topic, even to just express to yourself that you are 'recovering' and pleased with yourself about it is two-fold:

1. It again is a way of allowing your dysfunctional ego to, covertly, bring the topic up again and get you back on to it.
2. If you feel you are leaving him or her behind, you may start to feel guilty, sad or it may affect the way you feel about where you are at.

Know that, perhaps one day in the future you can go back into this, if you really want to look at the situation for any reason, but for now- while the pain is still somewhat active and fresh- you are going to leave it be and put your attention elsewhere. If you have struggled for a while with this situation you will know that no amount of digging, trying or thinking on this subject has released you from it so far. The way I dealt with it and I am suggesting you try, is to bypass it entirely.

Every time your mind pipes up with a reason to think, compare or dig at it, you must refuse; remember the steps we have taken together through this book.

Go back to your list, get into your box of tricks, follow

the plan and be what you are and be who you are.

It might be difficult, you may have to take yourself off the topic of the other 100 times a day at first but, whatever you have to do, be persistent and keep off the subject of him or her. Eventually, day by day it will get less. Will you be recovered and totally at peace over it in 14 days?...quite possibly not. I am not telling you that in 14 days I was recovered. However, 14 days of effort to step into my true self showed me: a glimpse of who I really was, self sufficiency and the road out of the loop of misery I was in. It allowed me to see a different way and that I could, if I kept following the steps and building my sense of self, be completely free again one day. I did and now I am. What more can I say?

I found my freedom and so can you.

"She opened
her heart to herself
and then the magic
happened"

The 14 day plan

*B*uy, make or recycle a small pad or notebook to keep your ideas and daily work in. You can also journal in this as an addition to the 14 day plan if you want to. It doesn't need to be anything special; it is what you put in it that counts. Make sure that you put your list and the work on yourself that you did in step 7 above, at the beginning of your workbook. You are going to be using this every day.

This plan is the simplest and yet most helpful list of daily things that I did that started me on my road to freedom and heartbreak free existence. Regardless of your commitments and workload, you should be able to manage it. There is a simple morning routine (5 mins), a wellbeing routine (30 mins) and a self nourishment routine (1 hour) and an evening routine (5 mins).

Morning Routine.

If you have no time to spare in the morning, you can do this activity whilst showering, washing or applying make-up. I want you to quite simply revisit your list and outline of yourself. Who are you? What are you achievements? Who are you becoming and developing in to? You don't need to be overtly diligent in the finest points of your outline every day...

What you are really trying to do is grasp and harness its essence; to feel that sense of hope and joy of possibility.

What progress have you made so far and where are you going? This will set your day off on the right footing. When you do have time, go back over your initial plan and make additions or adjustments as things develop and shift. Allow your vision of yourself to become really familiar in your mind, this way, your focus and ideas will start to become habits and your sense of self and purpose will grow. Once this happens, you will have your subconscious mind doing a lot of the work for you.

Wellbeing routine

Again, this can be done whilst doing other things.

1. Move your body. Take at least a 15 minute walk or any exercise of your choice

2. Listen to 15 mins of positive input via a podcast, internet clip or a book for example.

You can of course listen to something whilst you exercise or do other practical tasks in your day just as you can incorporate your exercise into other activities too. It does not need to be a 'special time' set aside. In fact, if you make it so, chances are it may be harder to stick to it and to keeping it in your routine. This is why we make it a very small and convenient amount of action to begin with and do it in the most fuss free of ways. If you do this, you will find it easier to stick to. If you already do at least 15 minutes of exercise and 15 minutes of positive input, make the effort to improve these activities or extend them. You can extend them by just spending a little longer doing it or improve the quality by making sure you are totally present and aware as you exercise or listen; instead of drifting off into a list of things you need to do or running through ideas and activities in your head, you can really focus on the words you read or hear or breathe and feel your body as you exercise.

3. Make a small change to the way you fuel your body.

You do not need to make a massive change; just a small one. Examples of acceptable changes:

- drinking a certain amount of water and carrying that bottle with you all day
- cutting down to 4 cups of coffee instead of 6.
- reducing your sugar intake

However, these changes must be small and a manageable amount of difference. I simply would not encourage you to make a massive change or start cutting something in or out altogether. The idea with the well-being challenge, is to be moderate.

If we make a massive change, even if it is 'positive', it is going to be difficult to stick to and perhaps painful. If it is painful and arduous, considering you are already feeling some degree or other of pain and suffering due to the heartache, you are unlikely to want to keep up the wellness routine. A small amount of positive over a very long time is worth so much more than a big improvement over a couple of days. The small positive change can easily be made permanent and is then buildable towards a bigger goal in the long term.

Self Nourishment Routine

This is going to be hard for some of you who say you have no time.

However, it is so important that you do make the time.

It might mean getting up earlier or giving up some social media time or TV watching time. But, for an hour a day you are going to do an activity that feeds your soul. What creative or enjoyable pursuits did you include on your list? What do you have in your box of tricks? What did you organise for yourself? I write every day for at least an hour. Before I was sure about writing, I would also collage, collect picture boards of inspiration and design, and watch inspirational films and documentaries. The key was I was filling myself up. I was aware of who I was and how I could nurture and grow myself, my talent and release my abilities into the world. That is the job of us all and this time is to help you identify yourself more clearly, focus on you and grow that part of yourself.

Evening Routine

Rather like the morning routine, my evening routine isn't a fixed meditation or contemplation that is rigid in its content.

All I want you to do is smile to yourself, perhaps as you get in to bed in an evening or as you are taking a few moments to yourself at the end of the day, and contemplate all that you have achieved today.

What made you proud?

How did your self nourishment go?

Did you read or hear anything that really inspired you in your wellbeing reading/listening exercise?

Also, revisit that sheet you made of who and what you are; just whatever of it you can remember (you don't need to physically study it). Notice how much more aware and focused you are on your own sense of self and your own ideas. Notice how you are already starting to grow and gather yourself back together. This evening routine is about self appreciation and gentle affirmation of where you are going. I would strongly advise you not to go over your list in detail or review your goals and ideas too closely for obvious reasons; if you do this you could possibly 'whip yourself up' at the end of the day when, really, you need to be winding down.

"She saw her magnificence and majesty...then the world reflected it back to her"

Journaling

Whenever you do it is up to you but try to review your vision and write something in your notebook daily. You can keep a quick journal or use some time in one of the other exercises. It doesn't have to be extensive but just keep yourself focused and aware of what you want and where you're going. Remember this is a time of growth and renewal but old habits take effort to change.

Notes On the Reality of the Plan

➢ **I cannot reiterate enough that you will need to stick at it.** All of the steps are very positive and talk very enthusiastically and optimistically for obvious reasons. This isn't to say it will be easy.

➢ **Don't be hard on yourself** if you try to do one of the exercises and it just doesn't work for you that day; that is ok. If you have tried, you have achieved. It will not work every day. However, if you can come back the following day and try again, you have what it takes to build and move past your heartache.

➢ **Do not be surprised if from time to time you feel it is a waste of time or not going to work,** once you have started doing the steps, or the plan itself, be disciplined and stick to it anyway. If it doesn't work, all you have lost is a few hours focusing on your own joys and talents over the space of 2 weeks. Even if it doesn't cure your heartache, it cannot be a detrimental thing! What I can guarantee 100% is that, if you don't follow through and do it, it definitely won't work.

➢ **Try it, work at it and put the time in to you.** You are beautiful, fantastic, unique and worth it. Most importantly, however it may feel at this time, you can and will move past this difficulty. My prayer, hope and wish for you is that you see in yourself your own magnificence and majesty; that you be easy on yourself and respect yourself for all you have endured. I believe you can and will conquer this and am sending you love and light as we move through this journey together.

Join me and the 'Spiritual Candy' community:

www.spiritual-candy.com

Love and Blessings Kat x

Get the free
"Awaken your Dreams"
video course and tools

by signing up to the Spiritual Candy community

www.spiritual-candy.com/free-video-course/

45739229R00035

Printed in Poland
by Amazon Fulfillment
Poland Sp. z o.o., Wrocław